Motivation

Motivation

Motivation is the driving force by which humans achieve their goals

Murfreesboro Writers Group

Copyright © 2012

An Anthology, titled *Motivation*
from The Murfreesboro Writers Group
with contributions from the following authors:
Dr. Robert Michael
Susan Ashley Michael
Deb Simpson
Matthew Watts
David Fann
Pete McNally
Ken Vanderpool
Amy Williams
William Visher
Chance Torrez

ISBN: 978-0-9848968-2-0

Publisher: Piney D Press
www.PineyDPress.com

Appreciation & Acknowledgments

To the very talented **Sandra Vanderpool,** wife of MWG member, Ken Vanderpool, who provided the cover design for this anthology:

Sandra graduated from the Minneapolis Vocational and Technical Institute with her degree in Commercial Art. She worked as a graphic artist for twenty years, first in her hometown Minneapolis/St. Paul, and also after moving to the Nashville area in 1976. Sandra takes classes and attends workshops to broaden her art knowledge and painting skill. Sandra lives and maintains her studio in Murfreesboro. Visit her at www.sandravanderpool.com

Thank you for sharing your talent!

To MWG member, **Susanne Hebden**, who dedicated funds for this project:

Thank You for your support!

To MWG cofounder, **Susan Ashley Michael**, who gave her time and dedication in reviewing, critiquing, and editing each submission, and the final manuscript; and to founding member, **Deb Simpson**, who compiled the anthology and formatted it for publication:

Thank you for your diligence & patience!

To the MWG members who could not participate in the anthology, please know that we missed your wisdom and words. **For our former members** and friends of the MWG, we hope to see you in our writer's circle someday very soon!

To the community of Murfreesboro:
Thank you for the culture that supports and inspires groups like the MWG

To Barnes & Noble, Murfreesboro:
And the many staff members and booksellers who have assisted us with meetings, book signings, and telling the community about our authors:

Thank you for all you did for us in the four years that we met surrounded by shelves of our favorite books! Although the changes in the store made it necessary for us to find a meeting place, you remain a part of the fabric of our group.

To Hastings Bookstore, Murfreesboro:
Thank you for your continued support of local authors. We appreciate the many book readings and signings that you host, and the professional manner in which you display and promote the books of our authors.

To the families and friends of the MWG:
Thank you for continuing to support us as we dedicate time to our Muses, and to speak to our characters, as if they sit beside us at the table.

Table of Contents
Contributors & Contributions

About
The Murfreesboro
Writers Group
(MWG)

The MWG

In 2007, the group began
An eclectic group of strangers
Now authors and friends

Meeting twice a month
Surrounded by the grail
The smell of printed inks
The sound of forming tales

We listened and we read
We stammered and we tried
To give the world the words we heard
From the muse deep inside

Since 2007, the MWG has changed

We lost our treasured leader
We lost some members, too
We lost our bookstore meeting place
But through all that, we grew

Some members published books
Others moved away
Some moved on to other tasks
Some remain today

Our mission is the same
To encourage and critique
To help each other find a voice
To help each other speak

We are and remain open to new members
Encouraging writers
Telling our stories

The MWG

By Deb Simpson

On the following pages, you will meet our talented members, and get to know them through their words and in their descriptions of what motivates and inspires them.

Our Theme

Motivation

For this anthology we chose the theme of **Motivation**

For that is the force that compels

Writers to Write

Painters to Paint

Musicians to Compose

Creativity begins with the Muse

But it is Motivation

That leads the Muse into motion

And allows the thoughts and visions to become

A work of art

Join us in celebrating ***Motivation***

Motivation

Many of us have no trouble becoming inspired to do the things we enjoy, it's

Only when we face the obligatory, inane, and irritating tasks we detest,

That we push back, procrastinate and possibly avoid altogether

Involving ourselves in the insignificant or possibly painful chores which have no

Value (at least to us), but seem to take a priority position with one who influences us,

And who might feel it necessary that they introduce 'consequences' for our resistance.

This type of response on the part of the influential person, although motivating for us,

Is not welcome, since it forces us to make uncomfortable decisions about trade-offs,

Or our needs, such as prepared nourishment, clean clothing, and other—desirable things.

Now, that being said, "Honey, what was it you wanted me to do for you?"

Ken Vanderpool

Motivation and Movement

Motivation

Moves us

To reach and grasp

Motivation

Moves us

To wonder and ask

Motivation

Moves us

To pathways unknown

Motivation

Moves us

To leave the safety of home

To Risk

To Realize

To Renew

Motivation is

The inspiration of

Movement

Deb Simpson

In Memoriam

Dr. Robert Michael

Founder
Murfreesboro Writers Group

Dr. Robert Michael

Robert Michael was a Professor Emeritus of European History at University of Massachusetts Dartmouth, where he taught the Holocaust.

Bob Michael

He was a Woodrow Wilson Fellow in Philosophy at Columbia University, and an NDEA Fellow. He served in the U.S. Army at the Pentagon and in Bitburg, Germany, 4th Missile Battalion, 6th Artillery Regiment, 7th Army. Following his service in the U.S. Army, he was an editor in New York City

Dr. Michael published poetry, more than 50 articles and eleven books, before his death in February 2010.

He also taught at Central European University in Budapest, Inter-American University in Puerto Rico, and lectured at the University of Vienna, the Ateneo Veneto and University of Venice, University of South Florida, Florida Gulf Coast University, Ringling College of Art and Design, Florida State University, and Middle Tennessee State University.

In 2007, Bob co-founded, along with his wife Susan, the Murfreesboro Writers Group. Find Bob's books @Amazon: http://www.amazon.com/Robert-Michael/e/B001H6GWI0

My Jewish God
By Robert Michael

Ven men sol got dankenfar guts volt nitgevyn keyn tsayt tsu baklogn zikh oyf shlekhts.

If we thanked God for the good, there wouldn't be enough time to complain about the bad.

My bedroom's ceiling faded away into infinity. It's single window took up almost the whole wall at the foot of the bed. Only one other piece of furniture found its way into the cramped room, a creaky hand-me-down bureau. Mother always forced me to bed before the sun disappeared behind the city of Hope's Massachusetts hills. Sometimes with a pot or fry pan in her hand. But this didn't mean I went to sleep. As soon as mother left the kitchen for her own bedroom, I found my flashlight hidden in the bottom bureau drawer and, under the covers, read and wrote. On old newspaper, I drew Plastic Man, my favorite comic-book hero, one of my Jewish God's heroes trying to mend a broken world. Plasman wrapped his enemies--Crab, Dazzla daughter of darkness, Fiend, Mangler, Raka the Witch Doctor, and Amorpho, Plasman's evil double--into gift packages and delivered them to justice. And he wrapped his infinitely extendable arms around his girlfriend Penny, the beautiful young woman with huge babooms.

I imagined my Jewish God or the Messiah was something like Plastic Man. When I grew up, I'd help God make the world a better place, what the Rabbi called Tikkun Olam, repairing the world. It was World War II and the world was shaking itself to pieces. God created the world as a vessel holding Divine Light, but this vessel shattered into countless shards. Jews like me had an obligation to help God--even a God that suffered in silence-- by raising the wandering sparks of light back to the divine. I wanted to be one of the thirty-six righteous, the lamedvovniks who helped God restore a broken world to its original form.

The single window at the foot of the bed looked out upon a single maple tree. In the branches of that tree outlined against the bleak winter sky I thought I recognized the dark silhouette of

God's bearded face. I prayed to that image, "Before I can help you, o Lord, please help me get out of Hopeless. Carry me away to the world where the freight cars go, to Atchison, Topeka, and Santa Fe, to Georgia and Pacific, to Baltimore and Ohio." I placed pennies on the steel tracks and after the train passed by retrieved them flattened into new shapes like I wanted to be. I envied the red-winged blackbirds flitting over the dirty creek beside the railroad tracks where bodies of bloated puppies floated by. The birds soared beyond Hopeless. One morning, I clambered onto a red caboose at the end of a slow-moving Boston & Maine freight train. But when it stopped again near the Square, I jumped off, tripped on the railroad ties, got a wicked walloping for dawdling home with torn and blood-stained pants.

God never seemed to help me, never helped the Chosen People. "Vos hostu zikh ongezetst oyf undz? What do you have against us, my father often asked, glancing up at the ceiling after reading about some Jewish disaster. "We were chosen only to suffer."

I decided to give my silent suffering God one more chance to help. It was my bar mitzvah year, 1949. With the war over, the pennant race between the Boston Red Sox and the New York Yankees was heating up. The Sox came from way back to catch the hated Yanks, but they needed to win the last game of the season to capture the pennant. "Oh God of my fathers, God of Abraham, Isaac, and Jacob, God of Moses and Ezekiel, Jeremiah and Isaiah, take my jackknife as my humble offering," I intoned as I tossed it into the creek alongside the railroad tracks at the foot of our street. "Please, please let the Red Sox win. Prove to me, o Holy One, that you're a good God. I'll do anything you want if you let them win." Alone in front of the family's tablet-shaped radio, hands clasped in front of me, I got down on my knees, something no good Jewish boy ever did. I offered even my self-respect up to God as a sacrifice.
Then I listened to the game. Every Yankee hit cut me. Every Yankee run bled me. The damn Yankees tore out my heart and dug their cleats into it when they won the game five to three. My incipient faith drained from me like a rip tide.

It wasn't until years later, after I graduated from Harvard University, served in Vietnam in the Marine Corps, after I was working as an editor in New York City for a half-dozen years, and strayed mightily from the path of Torah that it all came clear to me. It was a colleague about my age named Ira. Ira was a curly-haired son of the Torah like me. He rode a motorcycle to work from Brooklyn. Because he wore no helmet, I considered him quite a fool. I thought back to my mother's warning, mit a nar tor men nithandeln--don't do business with a fool. But this apparent fool convinced me that of course there was a God and He was, yes, not only the God of the Jews but also that He answered Jewish prayers. His logic was so impeccable, it turned me back onto the path of righteousness and Tikkun Olam.

What was the proof? After I told Ira my woeful story about the end of the pennant race in 1949, he admitted that he was also praying to the Lord, but for a Yankee victory. He explained with a broad smile that of course the Yanks had to win, as they did most years. They won because God was answering the prayers of all those millions of Jews living in Greater New York City, many more Jews than were living in Greater Boston. My Jewish God did, indeed, help the Chosen People.

Professor Michael, was one of the 1997 recipients of the American Historical Association's James Harvey Robinson Prize for the "most outstanding contribution to the teaching and learning of history".

We will ever miss your strong guiding hand, your ever present smile, your wisdom, wit and love of life.

An Orthodox Jewish Burial for Yeshua Ha Notzri, Jesus of Nazareth: A Burial Such as the Burial for Every Orthodox Jew if There Were Time and Space.
By Robert Michael

Yeshua's body was taken down from the cross, and until he was buried, his conscious soul hovered nearby. The women positioned his body facing upward toward heaven. As if Jesus were still alive, they bathed his bloody body gently, with three pails of warm water, his head first, his right side before his left, his front before his back, exposing only that part to be cleansed.

"Master of the Universe," the women prayed. "Have compassion on Jesus, this child of Abraham, Isaac and Jacob. May angels of mercy circle before your servant, hiding his transgressions so that he may tread with righteous feet into the Garden of Eden."

As if a newborn, they cleaned, washed, and dressed him, intoning: "I will pour upon you pure water and you will be purified of all your defilements, and from all your abominations."

As if he were still alive, the women sang to him from the Song of Songs, the holiest of the holy books. The words rippled through the air, fled across the ceiling, shuffled along the walls, eddied around the table, caressing his tortured body. "His hair is black like a raven," they recited, "his cheeks are a bed of spices, his temples are like pomegranates. His lips are lilies perfumed with myrrh and frankincense. His mouth is sweet. His speech is music. His hands are gold rings set with green beryl, his belly is bright ivory overlaid with red sapphires, his legs are pillars of marble. His love is better than wine. He is altogether lovely as are the cedars of Lebanon. This is our beloved, and this is our friend, O daughters of Jerusalem."

As if he were still alive, they cradled him in a hammock and lowered him three times into a pool of cold water. They read more: "My God has clothed me with the garments of salvation, covered me with the robe of righteousness as a bridegroom puts on priestly glory and as a bride adorns herself with her jewels." As if he were still alive, they dried him and set upon his head a turban, and robed him in the white linen garments of the high priest--Kohan Gadol--of the Temple of Solomon, mirroring the mystical robe woven of his good deeds. Thirteen times they wound a sash around his waist, looping the ends three times-- once for God Almighty, twice for God's Presence in the world, thrice for Shem, God's name itself--to invoke God's calling of the world into creation by His word. They placed on him a prayer shawl--fringed with six hundred and thirteen reminders of God's commandments, less one, to note that this holy object was no longer worn by a living Jew.

As if he were still alive, they gently layed pottery shards over his eyes to force his soul to focus on the afterlife, and tiny packets of Jerusalem's earth over his mouth and heart and genitals--the three sources of sin. They gently placed him, clean and dressed, into a coffin fashioned of soft pegged pine like the Temple of Solomon's Holy of Holies. Before closing the coffin, they begged his pardon for any indignity they had unintentionally caused him, and they implored, "May you be an advocate for all of Israel. Go in peace, rest in peace, and arise in your turn at the end of days."

As if he were still alive, the women sat by his side so that his soul did not feel abandoned during its difficult transition to a new reality. "Yis-gadal v'yis-kadash shemay rabah" began the Kaddish, the Jewish prayer over the dead that makes no mention of death but praises God and asks for peace, a sacred mantra of cadenced comfort assisting the soul's ascent to heaven, the sibilant rhymes and rhythms of Aramaic. While standing, each woman ripped her clothing downward in accordance with God's commandment, beginning near the neck of the garment. No one could tear hair or flesh because each and every human being was a child of the Lord. Like a worn-out Torah, they lowered Jesus into consecrated soil. Dust he was and to dust he would return.

The women intoned, "Shema yis-ro-el adonoi elo-heynu adonoi e-chad, Hear o Israel: the Lord is our God, the Lord is One. Blessed is his name, glorious is his kingdom, for ever and ever." The women believed they saw his soul, as every, single, solitary Jewish soul is perceived, now completely free of the body, taking wing toward heaven.

Susan Ashley Michael

Co-founder
Murfreesboro Writers
Group

Susan Ashley Michael

Susan Ashley Michael

Susan Ashley Michael writes poetry and fiction.

She and husband, Robert (Bob) Michael, founded the Murfreesboro Writers Group in 2007.

Susan's first novel, *Crossing the Bridge of Sighs*, was published by Twin Oaks Press in December 2011.

Susan loves to travel and is learning to copilot a seaplane.

An excerpt from *Crossing the Bridge of Sighs* follows.

See Susan's website to learn more about Cianfrusaglie...
www.SusanAshleyMichael.com

Life is just a bowl of Baci...

Excerpt
Crossing the Bridge of Sighs
Susan Ashley Michael

Del senno di poi son piene le fosse.
The graves are filled with hindsight.

As the vaporetto made its way along the Grand Canal, an underlying rush of sighs and murmurs blended with the lapping of water against ancient foundations. Haunting whispers that reverberated along the damp alleys seemed to be calling to me, one voice growing more insistent than the others. What was it saying?

"Marco!"

Without a thought about consequence, my injured heart leaped to respond.

"Po-lo," I murmured.

And before I could draw my next breath, a thick cloud of moisture gathered and wrapped itself around my chilled body like a heavy cloak. I brushed at the dense mist, willing it away, and told myself to ignore these beckoning shades and to focus instead on the zigzagging path of the Numero Uno as it continued along the Grand Canal's parade of glittering palaces.

Some say that Venice was created when an angry goddess tossed a bowl of sweets and it landed here in the lagoon, scattering shards of crystal and candy. I saw my life as a shattered candy dish and couldn't imagine anything beyond its brokenness. When Bernie first entered my world, I envisioned him as a noble Saint Bernard come to rescue me from the cold, empty vastness of my days. But he hadn't come to rescue me at all, only to use me as a cover, and finally to desert me, running off to become a dot in the distance, a period at the end of a long sentence.

Swooping into my field of vision, a boatman in a striped shirt and pressed pants turned his heart-shaped face toward me, and as he worked the long, single oar of his gondola with ease, I felt my own arms aching with the strain of having hauled Bernie's stolen luggage. Time to get rid of it, I realized, so grabbing both our bags, I debarked at the next stop and summoned the gondolier.

"Angelo," he said, by way of introduction as he pulled up, stowed the luggage, and offered his hand.

"Take me way out into the lagoon," I said, gesturing.

His eyes held a question, but he answered in a pleasant tone, "Va bene." Negotiating the choppy green water with grace, he hummed a barcarole, its rocking rhythm mimicking that of the boat. The tune lulled me into a more peaceful state until we reached deep waters and were quite alone. Then, recalling my mission, I grabbed Bernie's bag and flung it open.

"Into the drink," I yelled, my voice unsteady. "My husband's a no good cheating bastard, and I'm getting rid of anything to do with him!"

"Scusa?" Angelo said, his almond eyes widening as I plunged into the jumble of clothes, grabbing the first thing I could get my hands on. A silk scarf, the distant smell of aftershave and Bernie's smooth neck. Hugo Boss? No, Calvin Klein. I tied the scarf in knots so tight my knuckles turned white, and when it hit the water, it floated away like a glob of spilled paint. I raised my hand to wipe a tear, but my fingers now smelled of early mornings in bed. Back into the bag I went, this time pulling out a cashmere cardigan that matched the blue of Bernie's lying eyes. I tossed that, too, along with pricey pants and tailored shirts. Into the lagoon they all went. And finally, I heaved fistfuls of premium cotton underpants—the ones that hugged his shapely butt. When they refused to sink, I was overcome with fury and frustration, and made a move to grab the oar from Angelo. I wanted, more than anything, to poke at the revolutionary seamless pouch—and give a twist.

"Che pazza!" Angelo yelled, managing to hold the oar out of my reach.

The sleek vessel rocked wildly as I screamed, "Stab them! Do you hear me!"

"Madonna!" the gondolier moaned, shaking his head.

With a growl, I tugged at my wide gold wedding band, tossing it into the littered water. My eyes spilled with tears, and the lagoon's surface turned from choppy green to a timeless gray waterway of thousands of damp, shifting pages torn from discarded books, blurry-inked letters, diary entries, tragedies and stories that had promised a happy ending. Then I sobbed and sobbed until Angelo, his expression softening, offered me his neckerchief. He studied me for a moment as I mumbled "Grazie," and dabbed at my eyes. Then he tipped his straw hat, red ribbons fluttering, and answered "Prego," with an inflection that sounded more like "Pray, go!"

"The Accademia," I said, indicating the graceful wooden bridge. When we reached the bank, he helped me disembark, and I tried to return his neckerchief. But Angelo shook his head no, so I handed him one of my business cards instead. He looked at its logo, TRAVEL LIGHT, and grunted.

"Arrivederci," I said. See you around.

"Addio," he replied. Not likely. Then he pushed off and disappeared among the throng of watercraft.
,

IBSN: 978-0-9844354-7-0
Susan's website: www.SusanAshleyMichael.com

Scan QR code to access Susan's website

Flying on Fat Tuesday
By Susan Ashley Michael

Red barns and shingled houses
pastures dotted with black cows,
silver silos foreshortened, battered,
and specks of white stone
that mark the dearly departed.

On Mardi Gras, 2010
tinsel twisted at the window,
a party hat rested on the sill at Hospice
as you enjoyed a last taste of vanilla ice cream
from a spoon warmed first in the palm of your daughter's hand.

Below, a train's wake of converging lines meets
the sky's rim, and from the milky
fracture at the horizon
a glimmer escapes like the dying light in a closing eye
while I try to stay in the middle of the air
away from the edges marked by the ground, buildings,
water, and trees.

As for interstellar space—
I hold a vision of
"Heaven" on a movie screen,
piano notes falling singly
a couple escaping
in a stolen helicopter
that climbs and climbs, becomes a dot,
and disappears into the blue
while in leather seats
you and I are served the best spaghetti Bolognese,
from Federal Hill,
the two of us alone, holding hands,
in a theater
in Providence.

(first published in vox poetica: August 31, 2011
Nominated for The Pushcart Poetry Prize for 2011)

Deb Simpson

Founding Member
Murfreesboro Writers
Group

Deb Simpson

I Write

I write to remember
I write to forget
To share the shame
To engage, to protect

I write to honor the past
I write to uncover the fright
To reach beyond the pain
To seek the inner light

I write to discover joy
I write dark moments away
To step from shadow's grasp
Sometimes simply to pray

Deb Simpson

I write for another's honor
I write for another's strife
I write for another's future
I write to make things right

I am motivated and inspired
To write where I have been
Like a tree that yields to the wind
I write so I may bend

Deb Simpson

Deb Simpson writes poetry, fiction, nonfiction and children's books. She is the author of *One Moment, One Memory, One Motion,* a poetic memoir; and *Pink Place & Blue Blaze, A Special Edition,* a children's book. Deb has served as a Court Appointed Special Advocate (CASA) for children in her home town, and donates a portion of the sales from *Pink Place* to support CASA's vital work. *A Guide to Using Pink Place & Blue Blaze* is also available.

Closing the Gate, the biography of Deb's brother, Jimmy and his involvement with the Heaven's Gate cult, will be available in March 2012.

Deb's poems have appeared in literary journals and other publications, most recently in the *Maypop* magazine (Tennessee Writers Alliance). Deb is a frequent contributor to *The Watertown Gazette* and was recently featured on the Creativity Portal website with a series of articles for writers titled "Your Book's Bottom Line."

Deb is a founding member of the Murfreesboro Writers Group, and actively participates in social media, including *Facebook, Twitter, Goodreads, She Writes, Linked In, and Crime Space.*

Deb is the President of the *Tennessee Writers Alliance,* and judge for the 2012 Global EBook Awards. She is also a featured Amazon Author, Goodreads Author, and Lulu Spotlight Author. Deb is the author of the dynamic blogs: *Live, Love & Write.*

Deb's website is www.DebSimpsonBooks.com.

Motivation

Ideas impeach the avenues in my mind
Images impishly fly
Thoughts tangle with tattered tales
Themes texturize with time
Another idea emerges
Another story arrives...

My writing often begins in lyric, images in word and rhyme tumbling in a train of thoughts, to my pen.

For me, there is no "NOT" writing. It is as necessary as opening my eyes in the morning to see a new day. The ideas and images may be sparked by the simplest of events: seeing a baby smile as it passes by in its stroller, hands waving at anyone who is nearby. Or ideas may begin in the darkest of times.

One my favorite books, *The Writers Book of Wisdom* states that "Writing works as therapy, for you (the writer) and your readers." I know this has been true for me. What I read and wrote during the dark times in my life became turning points, toward new hope and new directions.

So, when others ask me how I can write so openly about my brother's suicide, and how it impacted me, I often use a phrase borrowed from a fellow writer and founder of the Murfreesboro Writers Group, Bob Michael, who said, "There are people who have normal happy childhoods (or lives) and then there are writers."

In America's early years, before technology took over our lives, families used storytelling to teach their children about their family history, their beliefs and their expectations. Now, much of that tradition has been replaced as our days fill with electronic images and words. Many of the stories of my family are forever lost, so I tell the stories I know and remember as a gift for my children and their children and the family yet to be.

I don't really write the stories
They weave themselves into my heart and mind
And I share them from my soul.

Because of the path I have traveled, I know that one person can
make the difference in the life of another in one simple moment,
by creating one precious memory, or giving one touch that
reminds them they are not alone.

Share the moments
Share the stories
Share your soul
And don't let fear stop you.

An excerpt from *Closing The Gate*, the story of my brother's
involvement with the Heaven's Gate Cult, and his eventual
suicide, begins on the following page.

Chosen or Condemned
By Deb Simpson

Cult or Christian

Charisma or Control
Divine or Delusional
Chosen or Condemned

Apart or Alone
Concern or Coercion
Riches or Rhetoric
Chosen or Condemned

Spiritual or Spurious
Thorny or Twisted
Shepherded or Steamrolled
Chosen or Condemned

Do you know?

Excerpt
Closing the Gate
Deb Simpson

"It's past time for me to go.
The precious spirits have long since taken flight. "

Excerpt from Jimmy's letter of 5/10/97 and his sketches of the thirty-nine members of his cult family who were involved in the mass suicide. The figures that are more prominent may be "Older Members," or simply classmates that were more significant to Jimmy. He did not say.

Wednesday, March 26, 1997
Tampa, Florida

As I watched the evening news, I did not know that the events of this day would lead to my brother's death. When the newscaster began to talk about a mass suicide involving a strange cult in California, I watched with only mild interest, until he mentioned the nicknames "Do" and "Ti." I watched the news video of Marshall Applewhite talking about Earth being recycled. His eyes were wide and wild, his eyebrows raised and fixed, and his overall mood excited. His words were filled with intellectual deals, biblical language, and a monotonous tone. He appeared to be working to control the display of his emotion, but the overall affect was one of cognitive dissonance. His emotions were not matching his words and message.

"Marshall Applewhite, known as 'Do' and his partner, Betty Nettles, known as 'Ti' started this group in the early Seventies." the newscaster began. I felt my heart racing, as I raised the volume.

"Nettles died several years ago and the group has been living a nomadic existence for several years, only recently moving to the Rancho Santa Fe area. A local restaurateur tells us that the group came in together on Sunday, just three days ago, and each of them ordered the same exact meal of salad, pot pie and cheesecake. "I shivered as a chill ran up my arms and, for one moment, I stopped breathing.

"The thirty-nine men and women were all dressed alike in black sweatpants and black shirts. Each had the exact amount of money in their pockets, one five-dollar bill and three quarters. Some of the men had been castrated, including Applewhite."

The newscast paused for a commercial and my mind raced with concerns for my brother. *It is the cult that Jimmy had been a member of. Did he rejoin them? Was he one of the thirty-nine?* I hurried to call my aunt.

"Aunt Kay, did you hear the news . . . about the cult that committed suicide?" I asked as soon as she answered the phone.

"You mean those people in that big ole house in California?" she asked. "Yeah, we saw it on the news earlier today."

"That's the cult that Jimmy was in! Do you know where he is? If he's okay?"

"I reckon he's okay. He was the other day when I talked to him. Besides, what makes you think this is the group he was with? He didn't say nothing to me and Mike about the group planning to kill theyselves. Just said he was in a commune-like-place for a while."

"I know, but he didn't tell you everything. It's them. He told me about the names they used, the leaders, 'Do' and 'Ti' and how they had nicknames for everybody that ended in 'ody'. Jimmy was called "Gabody" or Gaby, for short. It was kind of a joke, because he talked, or gabbed, so little."

"Well, anyhow, he ain't with them now, so you don't need to worry none. He's here in Atlanta. Not in California."

"Can you call him? He hasn't talked to me since I refused to send him money the last time he asked, and I'm afraid he'll try to follow them."

As I hung up the phone, I watched the pictures of the bodies being removed from the house in Rancho Santa Fe. I turned up the volume just as the newscaster began to talk about the cult's history.

"It seems that this group has been known by many names: *The Two, HIM* (Human Individual Metamorphosis), the *Transfiguration Monastery for Renunciants in Readiness for the Kingdom of Heaven,* and the *Total Overcomers.* "

I knew it. It is them. The Total Overcomers was the name on the card that Jimmy left for Mother when he joined the group. The Transfiguration Monastery for Renunciants in Readiness for the Kingdom of Heaven was the name on the tract that he had left with his goodbye letter.

As the newscast flashed the date and time, I realized that it had been exactly two years ago, on March 26, 1995, that Mother died of cancer. I wondered how Jimmy would see this coincidence.

The next day, Aunt Kay called to tell me that she had spoken with Jimmy and everything was fine. We would later learn that even as he said this, Jimmy was planning his death.

May 6, 1997

Heaven's Gate was back in the news. A former member had committed suicide as he followed them to TELAH (The Evolutionary Level Above Human). Once again, I wondered what Jimmy was thinking, how he was handling the death of his spiritual family, and how he felt about not being there when they went to that *Next Level*, as he had called it. I tried to call him at work, but was told he was out sick that day. I wondered how many other former members were thinking of 'exiting their vehicles' through suicide.

Tuesday May 13, 1997

I left work early, not feeling well. When the phone rang, I considered not answering, but something told me that I needed to.

I heard the sob in my aunt's voice as she spoke into the phone "I'm so s-sorry. I h-have to tell you this . . . Jimmy is . . .dead."

I sat on the end of the bed, unable to move. As my voice cried, "Oh, no . . . Oh, God, no..." my mind began to whirl with thoughts of my only brother. Large, sad brown eyes. Playing in the sand with his cars. Reading, or watching television in his room. Always alone.

It seemed to me on that warm day in May that the world was moving in slow motion, nothing quite real, quite true. My feet were unable to find the floor, my eyes unable to focus. The sounds of the outside world were muted and distant, as if they existed in a dream. I could hear my aunt's voice on the phone and my fiancés voice next to me, but I couldn't quite comprehend what they were saying.

I heard myself ask the questions: "When . . .Where... How... " And I heard my aunt answer, but I couldn't grasp her words . I struggled to picture the events she described and simultaneously tried to prevent myself from picturing them.

Jimmy had left a letter explaining that he had to leave. That he didn't intend to hurt anyone. He had placed a purple cloth above his bed, had dressed in black garments and new tennis shoes, as his cult family had done, had lay down in his bed, and placed a gun to his head. He died in the ambulance on the way to the hospital.

My baby brother, my only sibling, the little boy who was more like my son than my brother, was gone. I remember one moment of relief; that Mother had died two years earlier and would not have to endure the death of her only son. But that moment passed quickly, followed by years of grief.

James Edward Pirkey Jr. died on May 13, 1997. He was thirty-six years old, had never been married and had no children. He had placed a gun to his head, and reached for the Next Level, the place where he hoped to meet the precious spirits already departed.

Closing the Gate is his story.

USA Today was where my brother learned of the group who would later become known as Heaven's Gate. Because this was a pivotal event in his life and death, I was inspired to write about that moment, in the following poem.

USA Today 1993

Announcement of the last opportunity
Reading that one notice
changed my brother's life
and forever took him from me

He left his family of origin to walk with his family of choice; to
be part of their life and work-as Jesus to his disciples
proclaimed. "Come and Follow Me"

He joined the classroom and became a scholar of the Bible and
other group teachings. The boy who was shy and withdrawn
became a man who spoke to crowds with passion and zeal,
proclaiming a different way of life.

The hermit who was most comfortable alone became a nomadic
prophet, traveling across America, always in the company of
others, nevermore alone.

The overweight adolescent, lover of burgers and fries, became a
slim survivor who ate only what others chose for the group
experiments.

The cynical consumer of religious critics and alternate lifestyles
became an outspoken oracle of the one true path.
The talented artist of erotic comics and caricatures transformed
into an unknown soldier, a footman for the mantra, and put
away his pen.

The man who proclaimed that all preachers were paid, all prophets self important, became a fool in folly, his words before his change

This man was dedicated, devoted to the class; supporter of their search. Until his fears returned.

In a classroom filled with visions, Next Level visitors and dreams; walking amidst the brethren, visible but to him unseen, the doubts returned, and then he walked alone...again.

In his soul, he struggled to reconnect his beliefs to his life, his hopes to the heart so changed. He stayed true to many practices; he heard voices in his mind, and tremors in his truths. He stalled and stumbled through Alaska and Arizona, returning to his home state only after his mother had passed. Only when she lay beneath the grass could he acknowledge that he did not belong. Perhaps he should return to the classroom...perhaps that was his home.

When the thirty-nine faces appeared in the news, he knew what he must do. With shame, he wrote of his vessel's struggle against death, his human attempt to remain alive. But still, he planned telling no one, until he wrote to say goodbye.
He pulled the trigger and ended his life. In his words, he removed the vessel of his human body to allow his soul to depart the Earth and join his classmates on the UFO bound for the Next Level.

He followed his beliefs and I lost him from my life.

Now only a memory

USA Today 1993

Heaven's Gate Away Team Patch
Worn by the 39

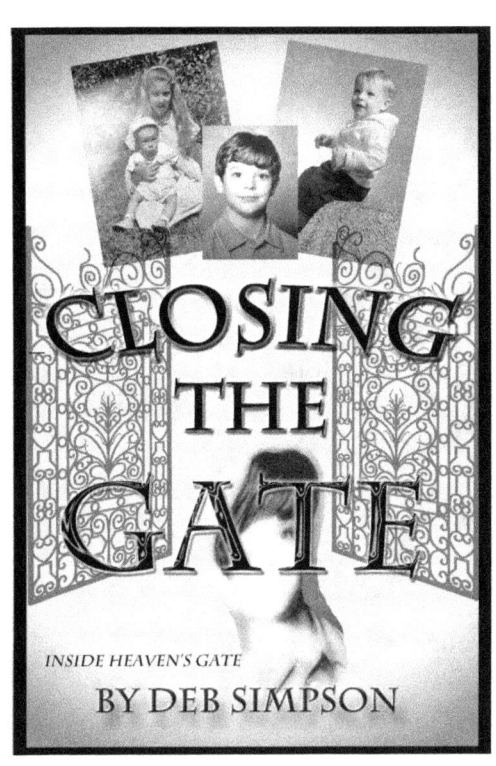

Closing The Gate
A Heaven's Gate Cult Biography
ISBN Paperback 978-0-9848968-0-6
ISBN Hardcover 978-0-9848968-1-3

Click on QR code to access www.ClosingTheGate.com

My inspiration for this poem came from a weekend of babysitting grandchildren and the communication failures that ensued!

Communication *is the foundation for connections, the way to understand others and have them understand us.*

C Caring

O Observations and

M Measures to prevent

M Misunderstandings

U Unknown

N Needs

I Inspiring discussion

C Concerns and connections

A Awareness of

T Time and our

I Impact on

O Others

N Named or not

As communes nurture the sharing of life

Words exchanged freely support solace in strife

Thoughts unrevealed simmer in the dark

Exploding expectations searing spark

Words on the wind
Crest and descend
In a peaceful exchange
Like the rhythm of rain

Vows and Voices
Concerns and Choices
Bartering Beliefs
Reasons and Retreats
Until center is found
In shared wounded sounds
Acceptance, Relief
And finally
Peace

It is the unspoken expectation that leads us to resent
The unknown desire that fuels the fire
The innermost flame not given a name
That results in the frowns and anger profound
So easy to ignore or postpone, yet so simple to prevent

By speaking our thoughts aloud
Communication
Fail to communicate and you fail to connect

Deb Simpson
www.DebsimpsonBooks.com

Motivation: An Anthology

June Hall McCash
Founding Member

June was unable to contribute to this anthology, due to her current publication schedule, but she is a founding member of the MWG, so we wanted to tell you a little about her.

June Hall McCash writes fiction, nonfiction and poetry. She is the author, co-author, or editor of seven books, including *Almost To Eden, Jekyll Island's Early Years, The Life of Saint Audrey, The Jekyll Island Cottage Colony, The Cultural Patronage of Medieval Women, The Jekyll Island Club,* and *Love's Fools.* June's poetry and articles have been published in numerous magazines and journals. She was recently named Georgia Author of the Year for her first novel, *Almost to Eden.*

June is a member of the Georgia Writers Association, and a frequent speaker, having done presentations for the Georgia Humanities Council, various historical societies, libraries, and universities, as well as the Georgia Center for the Book, the Georgia Library Association, the Jekyll Island Museum, and the Jekyll Island Club Hotel.

She is completing her second novel and is also about to publish a new nonfiction work. She also continues to write poetry.

Her website is http://junehallmccash.georgiawriters.org/.

Matthew Watts

Founding Member
Murfreesboro Writers
Group

Matthew Watts

Matthew Watts is a fantasy and science fiction series writer and a founding member of the Murfreesboro Writers Group.

He is currently attending Middle Tennessee State University.

"I wrote *Starlight* when I was sixteen. As my second series, I had many goals for this book. One was to implement the lessons I learned while writing my first series. Another, as a homeschooled only child, was to find a worthwhile use of my time. Most importantly, though, I wanted to create an entertaining story emphasizing the morals and values I was brought up to hold important.

Matthew Watts

Cavith is a young farmer who has lost his family and whose greatest wish is to preserve the family farm. He values honor and loyalty above all else. A man of integrity who has fallen on hard times, he is simply trying to figure out how to survive. His best friend, Javek, shares many of his ideals but places a premium on adventure and thrill. As a character-driven story, much of the series has to do with how their morals influence the world around them and vice versa. The adventure that unfolds around them tests their limits in ways they could never have imagined.

Excerpt
Of Knights
Matthew Watts

As Cavith awoke, he realized the storm was over, the sound of driving rain replaced by that of singing birds. Hesitantly, he rose from bed, put on his boots and made his way to the door. What he saw when he opened it drove him to the edge of despair. His fields were in complete disarray, almost entirely submerged, several areas under inches of water. Many of his tomato plants lay snapped in half, close to the ground. The corn, once halfway to his knee, now lay flat on the mud. His root vegetables were completely underwater.

He could see that any harvest out of the first crop would be only half his usual, that being an optimistic estimate. His hopes of finally getting back on his feet were all blown away in that cursed storm. He fought back tears.

Cavith forced himself to remember his father's determination, to make it his own. He set to doing anything he could think of to salvage as much as possible. He knew he would be facing a difficult winter.

He worked constantly, not even sparing the time to visit Javek, though his friend came to check on him every couple of days. Despite his best efforts, three quarters or more of the plants were dead or as good as dead, either by root rot or being too battered to recover.

He would be forced to spend every vendel gained from the first crop to buy seed for a second, and he would need to sell much more of the harvest than he wished to, in order to buy seed for next year. He was already rationing his food and considering what belongings he might be able to sell. He hoped to make enough kills hunting to ease his situation.

With a tender touch, he propped up yet another tomato plant. This one had managed to stay full and green while so many others were withered and brown. He caringly tied it to the stake. There was a chance that this battered little plant would survive and yield a good harvest.

"How goes it?" Javek called as he came down off the path from town and into the field.

"I would rather not discuss it."

A smile on his face, Javek said, "I know something that will lift your mood."

Laughing at the absurdity of it, Cavith asked, "And what might that be?"

"Get your father's sword, and I'll show you."

Reluctantly, Cavith tore himself from the field and fetched the sword. Together, he and Javek headed back to town. As they made their way along the path, Cavith wondered if his friend was about to get him into another one of his so-called "adventures."

Reaching the village, Cavith saw that everyone was assembled by the well. He headed off towards the gathering, fascinated by the sound of two pieces of metal clashing together. Javek stayed close beside him, grinning more widely than ever. An unfamiliar man's voice issued forth from among the assembled villagers, though the collective murmurings of those present made it impossible to tell what he was saying.

He stood in the center of the ring-shaped crowd along with his horse, facing Patith, the best at swordplay in the village, apart from himself and Javek. The stranger's clothes were dark purple, blue, and black, and were of the finest make. His forehead bore a long scar that extended up into his scalp, and a number of small scars crisscrossed the back of his right hand. A large purse hung prominently from the horse's saddle, along with several smaller purses. Both men stood with swords drawn.

With impressive speed, the stranger moved on Patith, executing a reliable yet all too predictable series of moves. Patith recognized it instantly, being one that Cavith favored on the rare occasions they dueled, and he managed to defend against it well. When the stranger entered his next series of moves, though, he scored a quick blow to Patith's gut with the broad of his sword, ending the match without wounding him.

"I never thought Patith to be foolish enough to waste his money fighting swords," Cavith said.

"Neither did I," Javek agreed. Handing Cavith a heavy purse, he said, "Take this."

"What are you doing?"

"Just stay calm."

"Who's next?" the stranger called.

"I'm not volunteering to go up there," Cavith whispered.

"I know. Give me more credit than that."

"Come!" the stranger called. "There must be someone here who can beat me! Fifty vendel to fight. The winner keeps all that has been wagered today! That's five hundred vendel!"

Five hundred vendel was quite a sum-nearly a third of a year's earnings for most of the townspeople of Predan. Still, Cavith could not understand how anyone in their village could spend fifty vendel on the challenge. The man obviously lost very rarely, and the people in Predan were not known for their prowess with a blade.

"Is there still one who will fight? Certainly, there must be one here who can beat me! One able to overcome me! Who will fight?" the man called.

"He will!" Javek called, jumping up in the air and pointing wildly to Cavith.

Suddenly, Cavith became aware that he still held the purse and all eyes were now on him.

"I told you I wasn't volunteering," Cavith growled, knowing that backing out would make him look like a fool or a coward.

"I told you that I knew you weren't," Javek said. "Think about your fields. I finance, you fight, we split it down the middle."

"Come, young man!" the stranger called.

Cavith walked slowly up and, after a moment's hesitation, handed over the purse, realizing that, though he himself had not put anything on the fight, Javek was risking most of what he owned.

As the man examined its contents, Cavith knew that this fight could be the death of him, as they were dueling with sharpened swords, being the reason that the stranger kept hitting with the broad side of his weapon. He felt apprehensive. The man hung the purse with the others, and Cavith cleared all irrelevant thoughts from his head.

After taking a few steps back, the stranger asked, "Ready?"

Shifting his stance to a defensive posture, Cavith replied, "Ready."

"Begin."

For a moment, they both stood motionless, until his opponent realized that Cavith was not going to make the first move. Almost immediately the man went into a speedy series of attacks, well thought-out and dangerous but ultimately simplistic. Cavith blocked each strike, making a point to memorize his opponent's form. Despite his skill, Cavith found himself backpedaling.

It took him by surprise when he realized his adversary was using a twelve-move pattern that he kept repeating. He moved faster each time, making it appear, to the untrained eye, as though he were improvising.

Using all his speed, as the man went into his fourth repetition of the series, Cavith slapped him across the face with the broad of his sword.

The man stopped instantly, a look of shock and of anger coming to him. For a moment, Cavith wondered if he would be true to his word. The townspeople applauded Cavith, glad to see that their village did indeed have a champion.

Without a word, the man sheathed his sword before slipping the purses of gold from his horse's saddle and handing them to Cavith. Finally, he forced a smile.

"I told you there was one who could beat me here!" The man sounded as friendly as ever, as much a salesman as a swordfighter. He went over to his horse and climbed onto the saddle. Barely had he gotten the pleasantries out of the way before turning his horse about and riding out of town.

The crowd dispersed and several villagers made their way up to congratulate Cavith. Finally, only he and Javek were left.

"Impressive," Javek said admiringly. "For a moment, I feared I'd done something foolish."

"Two fifty?" Cavith checked, surprised how heavy the gold felt.

"Unless you think my encouragement is worth three."

"Two fifty ought to do it," Cavith laughed, depositing the sum into Javek's purse.

"Celebrate with me?" He gleefully tossed his earnings in the air like a ball.

"I should get back to the farm."

If Cavith was careful with what he now possessed, he could probably buy seed for a second crop and make it through the winter. It was enough to start him planning in the long-term again.

"You and that piece of dirt," Javek sighed. "Celebrate with me."

"I've not the money for revelry."

"I'll see you soon?" Javek asked

"I'll be busy working on the farm for awhile."

"I'll make a point to drop in soon," Javek said. "See you then."

"See you then, my friend. And thank you," Cavith said, turning back towards the farm.

"Don't mention it," Javek called, no doubt turning to Trask's tavern.

On the walk back to the farm, Cavith's thoughts were filled with all the different ways he could get by on what assets he now possessed. He started a vegetable stew once he arrived back at his home, and decided to begin the extensive repairs the roof required. By the time the sun set, he was nearly halfway through. H e accomplished enough for one day and made his way to the ladder.

"I figured it out!" Javek called, startling him and almost making him fall off the ladder.

"Figured what out?"

"Do you have dinner on?" Javek asked, , a good sized pack on his back.

"Vegetable stew," Cavith answered, as he reached the bottom of the ladder.

"Good. I brought beef, bread, and ale," he said, a smile wide across his face.

"Come on in," Cavith said, making his way to the door of the house. He wondered if Javek brought ale as a celebration or to loosen him up for some kind of proposition.

Before doing anything else, Javek found the knives, cubed the meat, and added it to the stew. Cavith washed his face and hands with a cloth and basin of water, as Javek took out a loaf of bread and a small cask. By the time Cavith finished cleaning, Javek had poured two tankards of ale.

Cavith picked up his tankard, eyeing it suspiciously, unsure of his friend's motivations. Seeing him with the mug, Javek grabbed his own, held it out to Cavith, and said, "To the best swordfighter I know."

Unable to restrain a smile, Cavith knocked his tankard against Javek's. His friend took a couple of long gulps, while Cavith abstained. It seemed more than ever as though his friend had brought it to loosen him up. As soon as Javek saw that Cavith had not taken a drink from his, his smile shrank almost unnoticeably.

"Is something wrong?" Javek asked.

"I know better than to drink when you come to talk of something serious. What did you figure out?"

With a sigh, Javek said, "I'd hoped you'd drink some first. It would have made it easier on you."

"You mean easier on you."

"We do well when we go into a venture together."

Cavith knew his friend's unease was a bad sign. "We do."

"You have great skill with a blade."

"What are you proposing?"

"We have a chance to do something... something great." Marshalling himself, he said, "Lord Vlasiv's quest for Inion could bring us great riches."

"There will be hundreds searching for the sword," Cavith reminded him. "There will be experienced knights and treasure hunters searching. What chance would we have? Besides which, the title of knight and the recognition of noble blood go only to one."

"True." said Javek, "The chances of finding the sword are slim, but there's other money to be won than Vlasiv's. If we were smart, we would travel north, then northwest, towards the Plains of Grakoth, the last place the sword was used in battle. There are towns along the way. Even if you fight only three people in each town, you could make nearly a thousand vendel. The cost of two men living on the land for a year could not come close to that. If our search for the sword doesn't go well, we'll turn around and be back in plenty of time for you to plant the first spring crop."

"If we don't find the sword, you've only lost one year of farming, and I'll leave you with all you make in the swordfights. Even if you don't make a profit, you would have enough money left to buy all the seed you need for the first crop. Since the first crop is the more reliable of the two, you end up on surer footing. You win that way and I lose little, getting a chance to see the world along the way.

"If we find the sword, unlikely as it may be, then I keep the title of knight, the recognition of noble blood, the estate, the sword, and half the money, and you get the other half of the money and everything you've made in swordfights. I'll even reimburse you for the costs I incur on the trail. That leaves you with enough to farm for years, without worrying if it's dry or wet or stormy, and me with my dreams of adventure fulfilled. There's no way to lose."

The idea tempted Cavith. It was true that the spring crop was generally surer to bring a good harvest. If they left, he could potentially return with much more money, even in the absence of the sword. Knowing those two things made it very enticing indeed. Still, he hated the idea of leaving the farm.

"I can't go," Cavith said.

"Why not?"

"The animals, for one. They don't exactly care for themselves. Then there are the fields. I hate to consider the condition they would be in if I left for a year."

"You would make enough selling the animals to replace them when you return," Javek replied. "As for the fields, I'll help you if we don't find the sword. If we do find it, you can hire help."

"There's a lot of risk in fighting swords, Javek."

"You underestimate your skill with a blade."

"One year?"

69

"Less, actually."

Both were silent for a moment.

"You don't have to answer me tonight," Javek said, getting up and walking over to the stew, stirring it. "Just think about it."

Cavith finally sipped from his tankard. His head swam with all the possibilities the proposal raised. It was risky, but it held the promise of giving him more security than he had known in years. Sitting down at the table, Javek told Cavith about the rest of his day. Cavith paid little attention, though; there was so much to consider.

The meal was quite satisfying thanks to Javek's contributions. Though Cavith's ruminations left him picking slowly away, Javek downed his portion heartily.

They stayed up talking a while longer. Finally, Cavith retired to his bed and Javek cleared enough room on the table to lay his head down, not being of a mind to even ask about staying in Cavith's parents' room. Alone on his bed, Cavith's mind was overrun with all the possibilities. Sleep came with difficulty that night.

When awareness returned to him. Cavith looked about, surprised to see that all was still dark. Again, the question nagged at him. He rose from his bed and strapped on his boots. Cavith snuck out of his room quietly, trying not to wake his friend. He exited the house and closed the door quietly. It was at least a couple of hours before sunup.

He wanted to begin the day's work, to consider things while he had a mindless task to occupy him, but he knew there was not yet enough light to work safely. Resigned to the fact that he could neither begin his labor nor get back to sleep, he lay down in the damp grass and gazed at the stars.

Again, he turned his eyes to the same place he always turned them when he was troubled-to his star.

Watch for *Of Knights,* Matthew's first novel in the fantasy trilogy, *Starlight.*

Find Matthew on Facebook:
http://www.facebook.com/profile.php?id=1118478915

Lee Renick
Founding Member

Although Lee was unable to participate in the anthology, she is a founding member of the MWG.

Lee Rennick is an author, playwright, and Executive Director of The Business Education Partnership (BEP) Foundation for Rutherford County. The BEP was formed in 1988 with the help of the <u>Rutherford County Chamber of Commerce</u>. The purpose of establishing this foundation was to create outstanding schools by applying resources to bold ideas which would bring schools and businesses together in preparing our future workforce.

The Oregon native received her bachelor of science in Marketing from the University of Missouri and went on to work nearly nine years as a buyer and manager with Dillard's in Arkansas and Tennessee. She worked an additional four years in advertising and event planning in Nashville. In 1995, Lee joined the staff of the *Daily News Journal* as the Special Projects and Event Coordinator, but was soon promoted to be their very first Director of Marketing and Public Relations.

Since 1995, Lee has worked with over 30 education, arts and charitable organizations in Rutherford County. She is a member of Murfreesboro Noon Rotary, a 2001 graduate of Leadership Rutherford, and a founding member of Read to Succeed and Rutherford County CABLE.

David Fann

Member
Murfreesboro Writers
Group

David Fann

I came across a scripture from the Bible that I believe was written about me. It is from 1 Thessalonians 4:11-12 (NASB):

Make it your ambition to lead a quiet life and attend to your own business and work with your hands so that you may behave properly toward outsiders and not be in any need.

My motivation to write ultimately comes from God. I believe He is the One who gave me the ability to write, so I try to allow Him to inspire me with what He has created, whether it is through reflection or observation.

David Fann

Some poems may have been inspired by certain events, while others might be from listening to a song or reading Scripture. Others might have been inspired by watching a sunset on a beach or gazing into a valley from a mountainside. In any case, my hope is that my poems are able to inspire those who read them and that God uses them for His glory.

David Fann was born and raised in Murfreesboro, TN., and enjoys enjoys reading poetry. Although David has been writing for several years, he says that he only started being serious about it a couple of years ago. His first book, *Walking with God*, a collection of original poems, was published in 2009.

David is currently working on a second book of poems, as well as a short story. His literary influences include Mark Twain, Ernest Hemingway, and William Blake.

I wrote the following poem on October 12, 2010 while waiting to take a Math test covering truth tables. I was about to lose my mind!

I'm sure there's a story here,

But where do I begin?

Should I give actual facts,

Or factual acts,

Or do I just pretend?

Maybe I'll do some research,

Or make it up as I go.

I should probably present the facts.

But, really, I just don't know.

Walking With God
By David Fann
ISBN 978-1615792320

After writing this, I needed something to help me relax and also get rid of my headache from looking at truth tables for so long. This was written October 12, 2010 while waiting to take the test.

Ponder

Have you ever watched a sunset

With colors vivid and bright

Or gazed into a darkened sky

To count the stars at night?

Have you listened to the waves

Crash gently on the beach

Or noticed the butterflies

Always slightly out of reach?

Do you listen to the wind

Whispering through the trees

Or sit in a field of clover

And watch the dancing bees?

Do you stare at the moon

Wondering how life will be

I often think about such things

But maybe that's just me.

My next poem was inspired by a yellow finch hopping around in my backyard on a day when I had a terrible migraine.

The Little Bird

Have you ever heard
Of the bright yellow bird
That lived off the beaten path
He lost his head
And wound up dead
When he dove into a dry birdbath

This is a whale
Of a little bird tale
Whose feathers were yellow and bright
His bright yellow sheen
Could always be seen
Even in the dark of night

He kept his nest neat
And when he would tweet
He was heard from miles around
He would sing his song
As folks whistled along

A sweeter song was never found
A bigger party was never given
Even for those among the living
It really was quite a bash
Missed he will be
As well as his glee
When we listen as we open the sash.

The motivation behind this next poem came from my sons playing Challenger League Baseball in Mount Juliet, TN. This league is for children with disabilities and can be a lot of fun for the kids, as well as the adults. April 18, 2009.

The Ballgame

Take me out to the ballgame
Where the sun shines so bright
And the players play all morning long
As they each show off their might

Smell the scent of fresh-mown grass
Infield dust fills the air
They run the bases in a celebration of life
As the breeze blows through their hair

Everyone wins, no one can lose
That's how they play the game
Whether they run, roll, or hop around
They're all treated the same

They have so much fun; they're a joy to watch
It really brightens your day
You'll know when you see the smiles all around
There really is no other way.

Pete McNally

Member
Murfreesboro Writers Group

Pete McNally

Pete was born in Boston, and moved to Oak Ridge, Tennessee when he was three. He attended the University of Chattanooga and graduated from UT Knoxville.

Pete moved to Nashville in 1978 to work for the Health Department as a systems analyst; earned secondary math teaching certification at Tennessee State University. He then taught math at Spencer Youth Center in Nashville and at John Carroll High School in Birmingham Alabama, before returning to Nashville to analyze computer systems for Human Services. He later studied English at MTSU.

Currently Pete and his wife, Kathy, live in Smyrna where he enjoys reading, movies, music and writing short works. Pete says he enjoys the Murfreesboro Writers Group, and the members have improved his writing and inspired him.

Pete McNally

Pete is known for his unique dry wit and flash poetry!

Window

Raindrops
hang from bare branches
under a solid-gray sky
Chickadees, doves and finches
dance in a melody

(motivation: our back yard.)

Leaf

One orange leaf at a time
falls onto the grass
and dances briefly
before lying down

(motivation: our back yard.)

Hawk

On the telephone pole
a red tailed hawk perches.
Stopping the car to watch,
we talk too loud
and watch him glide away.

(motivation: driving on a country road)

Stay

A scent of holiness
woke him
and was still there
when the service ended
Still, he left with everyone

If it comes again
he thought
I'll stay

Maybe
beauty comes unexpectedly.
When will I no longer care
what anyone says?

You go on without me
I'm fine
I'll walk home
It's not far
I'll say

(motivation: the end of a church service)

Amnesia

When he woke,
he couldn't remember anything
Even passing moments
left no trace
anywhere in his mind.

Trapped in the present
The future, a void
No memories
to base plans or worries

Moments came and went
Great joy permeated
every impression
every act.

(motivation: writer's block)

Split

Heading toward the east
just before the split
there on the shoulder
a pretty red-headed lady
ejects herself
from the car's passenger side
swings the door shut
bounds toward the traffic
and thrusts out her thumb
very high
insisting that someone stop
and take her somewhere
away from he
who sits dumbfounded
in the driver's seat

(motivation: event on a highway)

Dancing Down the Street

Bob has that look on his face again
And now he's making those sounds
He's walking with a strange rocking rhythm
One step forward and then half step back
Now he's circling his arms in opposite directions
There's no music playing, except maybe in his head
He's listening to the universal symphony
Round and round he goes
Circling the room to the beat
Lord, I wish I could hear it too
He's opening the door
Down the steps he goes
I follow him; and my feet start following his
Down the driveway, onto the lane
Left onto the highway
A dark green van pulls up behind us
It slows
Pumps its brakes in time to our shuffle
All of us dancing down the street

(motivation: The Nightime Novelist by Joseph Bates)

Genie

George realizes he's made a mistake two seconds too late

The Genie is taking shape from the violet mist that drifted from the bottle

An odd genie though

He's wearing a suit and standing on the ground

But his smile is sinister, and he sounds wicked

As he says, "Your wish is my command, Master."

George wants to read again the fine print on the bottle

Opener of this bottle agrees to abide by all the stipulations of this contract

Among which are dread, boredom and the pursuit of illusion

But what the hay? Nothing ventured, nothing gained.

Just remember: once you open the bottle, you're on your own.

(motivation: The Nightime Novelist by Joseph Bates)

Find Pete on Facebook::
http://www.facebook.com/profile.php?id=1317318725

Ken Vanderpool

Member
Murfreesboro Writers
Group

Ken Vanderpool

Ken Vanderpool is a voracious reader who began to write in 2005 following an eye-opening medical procedure and an intimate encounter with his mortality.

Ken graduated from Middle Tennessee State University with his degree in Psychology and Sociology and an intense interest in Criminology. He has also graduated from the Metropolitan Nashville Citizen Police Academy and the Writer's Police Academy in Greensboro, NC.

Ken's first novel, *When the Music Dies* is presently under consideration by literary agents and he is at work on his second novel in the Music City Murders series, *Face the Music*.

Ken Vanderpool

He has spent his entire life in Middle Tennessee and proudly professes, "There is no better place on this earth." Ken currently lives in Murfreesboro, TN with his wife Sandra and their Cairn Terrier-ist, Molly.

Art by Sandra Vanderpool

The Wait
By Ken Vanderpool

Many years bonding their lives, partnered and content,

Loving and understanding, they waited on and for each other.

Incomplete when alone, they were a joyful set,

Grateful for the opportunity to enjoy life as one.

Time after time sitting at the window, she watched for his return,

Patiently for his homecoming from his labors.

Time spent at the windowsill waiting, she watched the shifting shadows,

As they marched along the empty street, time passing.

Thoughts entered her mind, unpleasant thoughts of missing him more than a while,

Not having him to complete her wait, no reason left for watching,

These feelings were more than she could stand.

Then she would see him in the distance, sigh, and be calm.

Some days delayed and knowing where she would be,

Devotion would swell his concern and love would quicken his step,

For fear that she would wonder and fret yet again at his absence.

He knew her thoughts, her heart; countless reasons why he loved her so.

But today she waits there still, knowing he will not arrive.

Time has changed both the window and the widow,

But the waiting, like the shadows, has shifted.

For he has truly arrived home, and now *he* is the one waiting patiently for her.

She is the one who is delayed,

But he does not share her wonder nor her worry,

Because he knows the time is soon when she too will come home,

When they can again be together and wait no more.

Inspiration

The collision of steel against steel and the subsequent crash of both vehicles against the concrete median wall produced an eerie sound. Almost two dozen road-weary tires pleaded for traction on the blistering summer asphalt, producing a frightening shriek. Start to finish, the destructive episode took no more than six seconds. The repair and healing from the collective damage, assuming it was possible, would require months.

Fingers on both sides of the interstate tapped rarely used cell phone key combinations in a frantic attempt to summon those trained to deal with life's larger tragedies. 911 operators were deluged. When phone lines lit up en masse, they knew; it meant a bad wreck with a lot of witnesses.

Dwayne Parker had recently stopped at one of the local truck stops to fuel up and grab some coffee. It was the only stimulant he ever used. His job was too important to jeopardize by using drugs to stay on his east coast to west coast schedule. He normally transferred the steaming coffee to his thermal mug before leaving the truck stop, but he was running behind because of a wreck near Cookeville and decided to return to Interstate 40 without delay.

Dwayne was in the process of pouring the coffee when he saw the car ahead of him change lanes. The driver made the quick adjustment in order to avoid a large ladder which was now stretched across Parker's lane, maybe fifty yards ahead. Slowing the truck with the exhaust brake, he checked his side mirrors and spotted cars along both sides of his truck. With the ladder approaching and cars on both sides, avoiding it was not an option. There wasn't room. There wasn't time. He couldn't stop. He had no choice.

Parker knew before his front wheels hit the ladder that his ability to balance the open container of hot coffee would suffer and his decision to hurry back onto the highway had been a bad one. He dropped the restaurant coffee cup and grabbed the steering wheel. As his front tire struck the ladder, the steering wheel jerked to the right forcing the scalding coffee in his mug to slosh onto his arm.

Attempting to stop the combined seventy-thousand pounds of truck and payload from entering the lane to his right, he over-corrected and plowed into the car to his left.

Charles Fleming was driving his sedan in the HOV lane oblivious to his surroundings when the tractor-trailer crossed the white line that was supposed to keep seventy mile-per-hour vehicles apart. The front corner of Fleming's car was caught up under the truck's tandem wheels and before he could comprehend what was happening, Fleming's car was forced into the median wall.

Startled drivers braked and aimed their vehicles away from the wreckage. One lady with medical training stopped and approached the vehicles, but backed away from the strong smell of fuel.

Informed by the dispatcher that the wreck was against the median wall, the firefighters knew from experience their best option was to approach from the opposite side of the interstate and cross over the wall.

When the wail of the fire engine's siren powered down, a half dozen highly-trained firefighters leaped from the large red truck and charged the scene. Parker was helped from his truck, physically unhurt outside the first degree burns to his arm, but no doubt damaged permanently by the incident.

Shawn Meyers, a certified EMT with nine years at the department, climbed the median wall and stepped onto the wrinkled hood of the sedan. Using a pry bar, he pulled the shattered windshield from the car and pushed it over the wall and away from the wreck. He leaned in and spoke to the driver, but received no response. Stretched out on the hood, Meyers grabbed the steering wheel and pulled himself across the dash and into the collapsed front seat compartment in order to get closer to the injured man. Shawn checked the man's carotid artery. He found a weak pulse from a heart continuing its innate task, still pumping blood through life-threatening wounds.

"He's alive!" the energized firefighter yelled to his companions. The announcement triggered an even quicker response from the others, including a call to Life Flight for air transport. EMT

Dominic Navarro was already delivering a trauma kit to Meyers so he could begin to stabilize the injured man for the trip.

The "Jaws of Life" is the telling name given to a collection of hydraulic equipment originally designed to extricate racecar drivers from their crashed vehicles. Within minutes, the metal blades of the hydraulic spreader-cutter severed the four pillars supporting the sedan's roof, and it was lifted from atop the car allowing the EMTs clear access to Fleming.

Forty minutes from the time the westbound lanes were brought to a standstill, and ten minutes after Life Flight's landing in the eastbound lanes, the critically injured man was secured to a backboard and passed hand-to-hand, up and over the median wall and through the rear door of the flying ambulance.

* * *

Now the fifth day since his ordeal began, Fleming was stable and improving. He had been recently transferred from the hospital's Critical Care Unit to a private room and was beginning to doze when he heard a knock on his door. He and his wife looked up to see two smiling uniformed firefighters enter his room.

Meyers and Navarro introduced themselves, but there was no need. Though he had never seen them, Fleming knew who they were. These gentlemen represented Fleming's Army of Guardian Angels who, less than one week ago, battled death in his honor, and won.

* * *

Many firefighters relish occasional hospital visits to meet the ones they almost lost. Seeing evidence of their success is their greatest reward for a job well done, and strong inspiration for tackling their next life-threatening emergency which they know is never far away.

Watch for Ken's new crime novel: *When The Music Dies*
Find Ken Vanderpool on Facebook !
http://www.facebook.com/ken.vanderpool

Amy Williams

Member
Murfreesboro Writers
Group

Amy Williams

Amy Williams has been a member of the MWG for two years, and writes poetry and short stories.

Amy often writes in a style reminiscent of Emily Dickinson, but adds her own flair!

She is originally from Washington DC, but graduated from Lipscomb University in Nashville and became a member of the Murfreesboro community.

Amy is a lover of fantasy fiction and all things vampiric!

With personal strife and fantasy in tow. The deepest of visions finds its way to the page once again. When you feel this deeply about life, love, and strife, the world sometimes becomes an unfamiliar place.

Amy Williams

Wrapped in ribbons as the mind and soul venture to a place
where the hidden veil engulfs us into the fantasy of our own making.

Amy Williams' writings are one of variety and vivid description. Born in Washington DC, she moved to Nashville to attend college and settled down with her husband in the Middle Tennessee area. She is an active member of the Murfreesboro Writers Group.

Affinities

Dance

Cast your spells through this electrified night

As spirits fly and sprites abide

Hither near to me my High Priestess

With raised arms I pray to my beloved Goddess

Reach down

Mark me

I begin to burn within

As your gentle kiss floods my soul

Filled with the spirit

I move

Taking in each affinity for my own

I am transformed

Full of the Goddess's incarnate

I am now one

Fire, Air, Water, Earth, and Spirit

No longer a wretched soul

Marked with the sweet spirit of the Goddess

Ms. Williams immerses herself in the readings of fantasy fiction.

Twisted Soul of Mine

Dear Lord

Touch

this twisted soul of mine

May I dance again to thy sweet song

Fallen in this realm's divide

I lie crumpled and dying

Shall it be death or blood that cross upon these hands

Before heaven's light is shed upon me once again

Blinded forever in darkness

These stale putrid mummies haunt me

Past the gates of hell

Father

Hast thou forsaken me?

With raised arms

I beg

for your answer

Save me

Tearfully I fall lifeless on this frozen and thorny ground

Sensations begin to dance

like feathers around me

Lifting my head

I now see the glories of the heavens before me

The angel of the Lord encircles his mighty wings around me

With burst of angel's light

I can hear the heavens rejoice

Golden is the light

From the holy temple in the sky

Laughter and songs are heard from above

You brought me to the water of life

Again I will drink

I took your hand

You led me to walk until our reflections became one

No more tears

No more pain

Cleansed by a wave of redemption

Arm in arm

We pass through the gates

To the place we can truly call HOME!

Savage Freedom

Enter the sick and warped fairytale vision of a place called home

Prickly words daunt these jagged halls as they permeate from a wrinkled, angry face

These should be those of the heavenly father's should they not?

The daily run around

The chase around

The never-ending run around

Caught at every turn like a butterfly in a net trying to get out

Entrance to those premises that door or else

The constant nasty and ugly request

Right this instant, or you know what

The ever-present chastening rod

Used to break the weary and the weak

Shepherd, see to the flocks

Not to run them off the cliff

Hear its song

As it releases its wicked putrifications

As the devil's advocate plays its perfumed dance

Every day and night of the week

Weeping alone in this tank of woeful dreams

A pit of tattered shreds that lie upon the floor

Hidden light shines where this broken heart and ravaged soul take refuge

Away from this deplorable savage way of living

Taking what is left of this person standing in the mirror

Glancing once again

A bag in each hand, then off, never looking back

The soul is finally free and leaps on angel wings with speedy flight.

In the next poem, Ms. Williams shares her conflicts between light and certain darkness.

Dawning of a New Day
Dedicated to my teachers at Tennessee Rehabilitation CTR

As the sun rises, we watch the dawn of a new and glorious day
The question lies in wait
What is in store for us today?
We begin our bright new morning in search of accomplishments
and rewards
for the difficult tasks we will set out to do

Entering a world of hard work and endless emails, buried by a
laundry list of things we must do
Never knowing what is hidden beneath our regimented patterns
For it is here that you win and lose it all to play the game in the
real world

Stepping through the plate glass window in search of a better life
a higher sense of self
In the process, we ignore the person frozen deep within
Daily fighting harder and harder to be the king, but end up
tired and shriveled within

You introduce yourself to a new place, one of understanding,
a place of belonging
Where others share the struggles of life in the same fashion as
you

113

So you make it your new home, but unbeknownst to you
change is on the way

Hustling along just like any other day, but the same stresses
of life seem to fade away
There is something special here, a feeling of home
So joy and laughter come to visit you once again, and all the
while
the rest of the secret lies hidden within

The daily struggle is still hard, but here it is, all worthwhile
Amazing confidence grows that was never there before and
finally you think to yourself, could this be real or just a dream?
Pushing harder on and on to see, what other things might come
bearing greater possibility

For the progress has come so far and so great
The hidden cocoon opens up transforming into a butterfly
Joyous peace with great sense of self hath come, but are we
ready to jump and run
We take our practice step to see if indeed we are ready
The time is nearing to say our goodbyes
The journey has been long, but an interesting one
We are now ready for launching ourselves back to the real world
So we assess what we have given away and what we have
received

For in the mirror stands a new person, one of hope, courage and
self-confidence

Ready to take the steps we never knew we could make
So the butterfly opens its wings and takes flight among with the other
winged creatures that sail to meet their new destiny

Turning to say a final goodbye
So filled with joy and thankfulness for all that we have received
Never forgetting the angels that have so lovingly watched over us
Stepping out with great happiness and optimism, we are so
blessed for the opportunity to have been a part of a unique and
amazing place

For I entered a stranger and came out someone I once knew
Therefore, such transformation could only have been possible
from such dedicated teachers who watched over me all the while
Everyday I will be thankful to have been part of a place that brings
forth so much good
For you will always be my heart and home, my sweet TRC!

Find Amy Williams on Facebook:
http://www.facebook.com/profile.php?id=1348921381

William Visher

Member
Murfreesboro Writers
Group

William Visher

William Visher is the owner and operator of Visher Ink Publishing, a business that specializes in all types of freelance writing services.

William earned his B.S. degree in Human Ecology: Early Childhood Education: PreK-4 from UTC (Go Mocs!).

He went on to get a M.Ed. in Early Childhood Education from the University of West Georgia and an Ed.S. in Curriculum and Instruction from Lincoln Memorial Universi ty in Harrogate,TN. He is also a certified reading specialist.

William Visher

He taught developmental writing at Dalton State College and now does freelance writing from his home in Murfreesboro.

What is Art?
By William Visher

One of my favorite quotes regarding art is by Ralph Waldo Emerson who says, "Art is the path of the creator to his work." Another is by Elbert Hubbard who philosophizes that "Art is not a thing: it is a way." As I began to reflect on what I "know" about art and about what inspires and motivates me, I realized that art was at once a process as well as a product. As a life-long participant in various aspects of the creative arts—school art classes, museum visits, community actor/director—I have been involved in both the process of creating art—material gathering, material preparation, media manipulation—and the product itself—an ashtray, a play, a greeting card, an interpretive dance. In a way, the artist is a part of the media used to create art. This is especially true in dance or in live theater where the human body is the medium of expression.

We know that art exists because it does. However we choose to define it; people have and will continue to use different ways to tell their stories. They will continue to interpret the world and reactions to that world. Even children from an early age seem to manifest a creative impulse through drawing in the sand, stacking blocks, and making mud pies. They do this even before they write or speak. In fact, children are taught in school to distinguish between colors and shapes before they can read and write.

According to Webster's, aesthetics is the branch of philosophy dealing with the nature of beauty, art, and taste and with the creation and appreciation of beauty. We have always heard that beauty is in the eye of the beholder—what one person finds beautiful or appealing, another simply does not. Therefore, aesthetics can play a part in art making only subjectively. The artist has to decide from a variety of angles how to create or recreate the product. From there, the artist has to decide how to get to his artistic destination.

In the broadest sense, art is not always a physical thing. As I stated before, it is also the process of creating, though you may have to use physical objects. For instance, a play uses physical things like people and props to get across non-physical ideas and concepts.

Both imagination and creativity play a part in art making. What you want your product to "look like" is a function of the imagination that goes into it as well as the creative process used to produce it. We use art for a variety of reasons. We use it to learn about our creative expressions, and to learn from our past. Art holds further value for us such as material, intrinsic, religious, patriotic, and symbolic.

The difference between creating and making is origin. Creating suggests originality while making suggests that you reorder or copy. To create is to bring forth something heretofore not observed.

Art is the process of creating, recreating, and/or redefining animate or inanimate objects or ideas into an observable form.

Everything and Nothing
By William Visher

Everything is all there is.

Everything is all there.

Everything is all.

Everything is.

Everything is nothing.

Nothing is everything.

Nothing is.

Nothing is all.

Nothing is all there.

Nothing is all there is.

William's upcoming Book

The Best Little Five-Minute Business Advice in Murfreesboro
ISBN: 978-1-257-77077-9

I went for a walk in the fall
By William Visher

I went for a walk in the fall,

and that is not all.

I went across and down, over and around,

above and upon, across and among.

In the fall.

I saw fall and smelled fall and heard fall

and was touched by fall.

I went for a walk in the fall.

William also performs in local stage productions
Look for William on Facebook:
http://www.facebook.com/profile.php?id=100001254374166

Visher Ink
PUBLISHING

William's website: www.VisherinkPublishing.com

Chance Torrez

Member
Murfreesboro Writers
Group

Chance Torrez

Chance Torrez is a native Texan now residing in Middle Tennessee. At only twenty-two, he hopes his imagination makes up for his notable lack of experience in the world and writing at large. When he isn't writing those cute little stories of his, he spends his time shilling out cell phones.

His motivation? Ah, dreams. The great mystery of this or any generation. Are they random synapses firing late at night? The subconscious reaching out to us? Or, some cosmic force impressing upon us visions to be fulfilled? Or perhaps some combination of the above? Whether we follow them with mad passion or let them wither and die on the vine, they are undeniably an intrinsic part of the human

Chance Torrez

experience. They move us; they haunt us; they elate us; and motivate us. And therein lies the moral of the story: Follow your dreams. Because the River of Night, like many things in life, is swift and wild and does not pause.

River of Night
By Chance Torrez

Marion Atwell can't sleep.

It isn't so much that sleep remains an elusive creature never to be found as it is that she refuses to acknowledge its existence. The dreams are getting more intense, more vivid, more irresistible. They must be stopped.

So, instead she lies awake in bed next to the man who calls himself her husband as he mumbles another name that is not hers.

She can never be like him. She cannot afford the temporary pleasure her dreams attempt to thrust upon her. It's dangerous for her to think about the thing she wants most.

Even now, the thoughts flood her mind, pulling her under: slender arms wrapped around her waist. The sweet smell of perfume, soft breasts pressing up against her own. Long, golden hair tangled in her fingers. Full lips caressing her neck.

These are ideas she cannot dwell upon. Impulses long cast aside. Desires stirring inside of her. Thoughts that keep her awake in fear.

She holds her consciousness prisoner in this world of pain and disappointment until it reforms or dies altogether.

James Atwell tosses and turns.

He drinks deeply from dream's full cup.

He follows after the woman of his dreams.

That moment, long ago, when she offered him herself and the world; they always begin in that café on Logan Avenue. The moment that shaped his life more than any other.

This time, he isn't indecisive, isn't scared of what uncertain future lies ahead of them. This time, they travel the world, his love and he. They toss and turn on the ocean. They are beautiful and young. He feels strong and sure of himself.

The slow degradation of his body is never felt here. The years of regret and settling for what was, in his mind, safe, are not acknowledged. Here, they only speak in song. Singing: "All is well. All is well." As they toss and turn.

Across the street and four doors down, the man named Rashawn Evans walks the streets alone.

He knows he shouldn't, but he can't rest. He's been held, alone, in a room long enough. He's been held in his mistake long enough.

He dreams, not as many dream- just the same as all dream. He dreams of freedom.

He wishes to find a certain, frightened old man and atone for it all. He wishes for a better city, a better education, a better father, a better life. He dreams of the land of missed opportunity. A land another man like himself dreamed of once.

No, not like him. That man with the great voice had never committed to violence the way Evans had. Had never battled his conscience in the night. Never had to take long walks through the worst parts of town in the hopes of finding the ghost of regret and laying him to rest.

Rashawn dreams of waking of up from the nightmare he's created. He dreams of letting go of a gun, still cold and unused. He dreams of a God who, he is told, can forgive.

In a dark alley, hidden from sight, a man dreams of all he has lost. His home. His childhood. His parents. His dog. His dignity. His voice. He dreams of these often, but they hold no such special place as when he dreams of what he misses most.

Tommy O'Doyle. Erik Bostra. Francis Devine. Miguel Castaneda.

Joshua Rosenthal.

Names.

He dreams of names. Their wonderful sound filling his mind.

Each his own. Each calling out to him.

Jackson Brown.

He's lost his somewhere. Somewhere years ago.

Bernard Livingstone.

He dreams of someone, someday calling him out by a name.

Someone who recognizes him. Someone who sees him.

Gregory Goforth.

He dreams of a forest of names, each one so high and out of reach.

Asif Bahar.

All but one.

 John Doe.

 He watches the names fall easily from the many trees, and splash across the toes of those like himself: hungry for names.

Up the street, David McKenna sits in front of his computer and attempts to get it all down.

He has to write. He needs to tell a story. He is drowning in a sea of thoughts, unsure of where to begin.

He's had a dream. It would make a good story, he thinks. He can't waste it.

He'd heard someone tell him once that the mind was a woman. They told him that every thought, every dream, every notion had come from the woman within.

The mind, she is pregnant. Every hour she gives birth. Every night the labor pains shock us awake. And to hold them in, to deny them life, to dismiss them, is an abortion.

David thinks about this a long time. He can't decide on it, but some part feels so deeply true.

He needs to deliver. Here in the dark. Here in this holy quiet. He needs to get it all down.

He imagines an answer, dreams of recognition, and envisions a world with fully realized hopes and aspirations. He contemplates an existence without hesitation or second thoughts; a time worthy of his thoughts. He dreams of justice and love and freedom. He dreams of a land far off, yet increasingly close-by.

He is writing it all down. He's giving it all away. He's releasing the life he holds within himself. And prays to God it will not be still-born.

Across town, Jacqueline Meister wakes with a start.

Beads of sweat and tears roll down her face.

She's had a dream unlike any before.

She stifles a scream and instead, breaks into a sob.

She can hear them all: All the broken thoughts of the night. All the unrealized hopes and fears. All the frail, inchoate dreams grasping at her as they follow the river of night, desperate for a home. Groaning for birth.

"It's an abortion," she hears one whisper. "To let them go, to dismiss them."

An abortion.

God, they know. They see.

Jacquie tries to reach out and pull them back, make them her own. She calls after them.
She can still do it, she thinks. She may have given up hers long ago, but she can still carry. She can hold one close. She can bring them back from the edge of endless night. She can save them, nurture them, bring them to life.

She watches as they float away.

"I'm sorry," she cries. "I can do it this time. I changed my mind. I'm ready now. I'm sorry."

Somewhere deep within, her abdomen wrenches and she falls to the ground in pain.

She looks down and sees herself covered in blood. And suddenly she feels emptier than ever before.

Murfreesboro Writers Group

The MWG membership numbers approximately 25

We are
>Poets
>Novelists
>Journalists
>Technical Writers
>And more...

We write in a variety of genres
>Literary Fiction
>Fantasy & Science Fiction
>Historical Fiction
>Biography
>Memoir
>Mystery & Crime
>How To & Self Help
>Inspirational & Christian Literature
>Children's Books
>Young Adult Literature
>And more...

We have many published authors among our ranks.

By 2012, MWG members will have published more than 80 books!

We do what we love, and we love what we do!

To our Readers

Thank you
for spending time with our words

We hope you enjoyed our collection
of poetry and prose, and
our thoughts on motivation

The Murfreesboro Writers Group

Would you like to know more about the
Murfreesboro Writers group?

Find us on Facebook

http://www.facebook.com/pages/Murfreesboro-Writers-
Group/137536252974939

Check out our Blog!

http://murfreesborowritersgroup.blogspot.com/

Many of our members are available for speaking engagements
and special projects!

To order additional copies of
Motivation:

Please contact the publisher, Piney D Press:

Web: www.PineyDPress.com

Mail: PO Box 332911, Murfreesboro,TN 37133

Discounts are available on bulk purchases
of this book

Special books or book excerpts can be created
to fit special needs.

www.ingramcontent.com/pod-product-compliance
Lightning Source LLC
Chambersburg PA
CBHW060425260626
47161CB00005B/1789

* 9 7 8 0 9 8 4 8 9 6 8 2 0 *